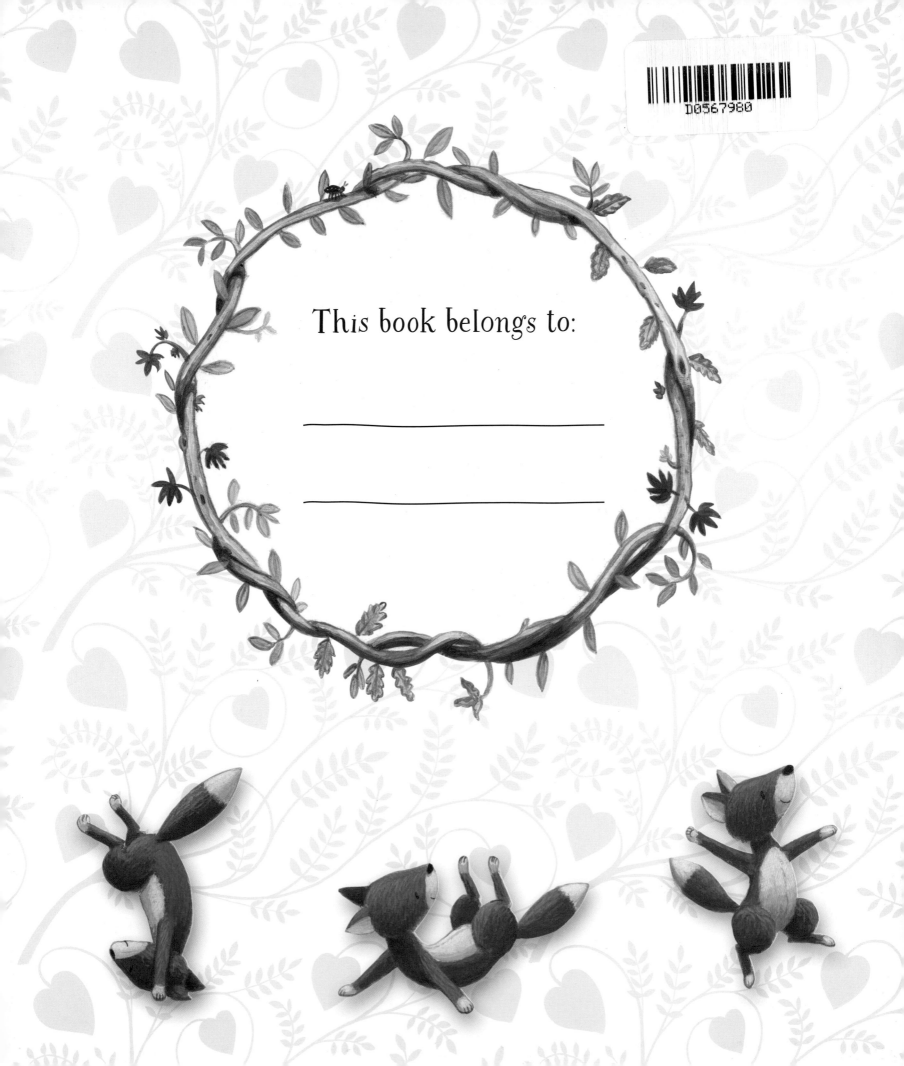

This book belongs to:

_____

_____

For my children,
forever. ~ D.C.

Per Mattia e
Samuele. ~ R.J.

Written by Dawn Casey
Illustrated by Russell Julian

First published 2016 by Parragon Books, Ltd.
Copyright © 2018 Cottage Door Press, LLC
5005 Newport Drive, Rolling Meadows, Illinois 60008
All Rights Reserved

10 9 8 7 6 5 4 3 2 1

ISBN 978-1-68052-547-2

Parragon Books is an imprint of Cottage Door Press, LLC.
Parragon Books® and the Parragon® logo are
registered trademarks of Cottage Door Press, LLC.

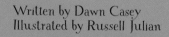

The Way I Love You

PaRRagon.

I love you the way the sun rises ...

... this day and every day.

I love you the way the old oak grows ...

... sure and strong.

I love you the way the leaves dance ...

... with dizzy delight.

I love you the way the spring bubbles …
… flowing and growing.

I love you the way the birds fly ...

... sky-high and soaring.

I love you the way the river runs ...

... light and laughing.

I love you the way the waterfall roars ...

... thunderous and wondrous.

I love you the way the rainbow shines ...

... joyful and jubilant.

I love you the way the clouds drift ...

... drowsy and dreamy.

I love you the way the great mountain stands ...

... unshakable, unquakable!

I love you the way the sun sets ...

... this day and every day.

I love you the way you are ...

... now and forever, with all my wild heart.